CHARLIE BROWN'S 'CYCLOPEDIA

Super Questions and Answers and Amazing Facts

Featuring People
Around the World

Volume 10

Based on the Charles M. Schulz Characters

Funk & Wagnalls, Inc.

Photograph and Illustration Credits: American Airlines, 476 (bottom); © Marc and Evelyne Bernheim/Woodfin Camp & Associates, 460, 463, 464 (bottom), 465; The Bettmann Archive, Inc., x; David G. Brown, 451, 452, 453, 454, 455, 456; Russell Burden, 478; Philip Dion, 470, 472 (top), 474; Japanese National Tourist Organization, 476; George D. Lepp/Bruce Coleman, Inc., 438; Mexican National Tourist Council, 476; NFB Photothèque, photo by J. Feeney, 444 (bottom); NFB Photothèque, photo by Gabriel Gely, 445 (top); NFB Photothèque, photo by Kurt Kammersgaard, 448; NFB Photothèque, photo by Scott Miller and David Hiscocks, 443; NFB Photothèque, photo by Terry Pearce, 447 (bottom left); NFB Photothèque, photo by D. Wilkinson, 444 (top), 445 (bottom), 447 (top right and left, bottom right); Holly Pittman, 461; United Nations, 472 (bottom), 473 (top); United Nations/FAO/H. Null, 469; United Nations/Kay Muldoon, 464 (top); United Nations/NAGATA, 462; United Nations/Philip Teuscher, 471; United Nations/Wolff, 473 (bottom); Dennis W. Werner, 435, 436, 437, 439; © Adam Woolfitt/Woodfin Camp & Associates, 459.

A large part of this volume was previously published in *Charlie Brown's Fourth Super Book of Questions and Answers.*

Introduction

Welcome to volume 10 of *Charlie Brown's 'Cyclopedia*! Have you ever wondered what the most commonly eaten food in the world is, or whether there really is an "abominable snowman," or how Eskimos keep warm? Charlie Brown and the rest of the *Peanuts* gang are here to help you find the answers to these questions and many more about people around the world. Have fun!

How People Live in the Rain Forest
The Amazon Indians of Brazil

What is a rain forest?

A rain forest is a very warm, very rainy place where many trees grow. Because of the rain, the trees grow tall and close together. The covering of treetops is so thick that it blocks the wind. The air is still and uncomfortable. The thick treetops also keep sunlight from reaching the ground. Most plants need sunlight to live. So in much of the rain forest, few low plants can grow. It is quite easy to walk through these areas.

A rain forest has more than a lot of trees. It also has many different kinds of animals. These include noisy birds, hungry crocodiles, anteaters, lizards, snakes, and big cats called jaguars.

Unfortunately, the list also includes thousands of different kinds of insects. Army ants eat anything that doesn't move out of their way. Certain mosquitoes give people diseases that can kill them. Sweat bees crawl into people's ears and noses. Ticks and flies bite their skin.

Is a rain forest the same as a jungle?

No. A jungle is part of a rain forest—the thickest part. It usually grows up in places where people have cut down the tall trees. Then many ground plants grow quickly. In fact plants grow on, around, and over one another. They tangle into each other. Because of this, a jungle is a very hard place to walk through.

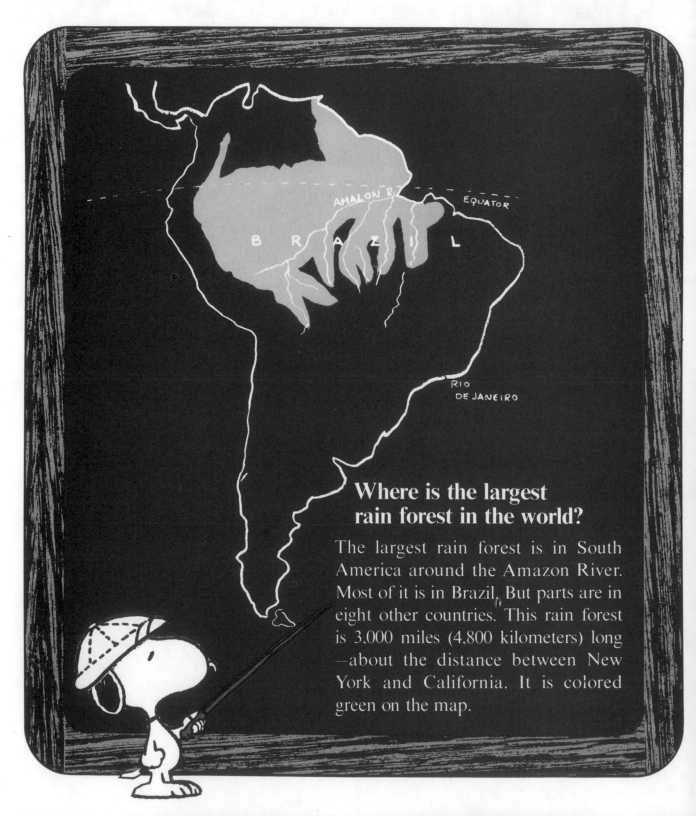

Where is the largest rain forest in the world?

The largest rain forest is in South America around the Amazon River. Most of it is in Brazil. But parts are in eight other countries. This rain forest is 3,000 miles (4,800 kilometers) long —about the distance between New York and California. It is colored green on the map.

Who lives in the Amazon rain forest?

Tribes of people we call Indians. These people are distantly related to the Indians of North America. But they look very different. They have darker skins and shorter bodies than North American Indians. Because they live in a rain forest, their way of life is very different from those Indians who live in Arizona, California, or Maine. Their languages are different, too.

Until recently, the Amazon Indians lived exactly as their ancestors had thousands of years ago. The rain forest kept them separated from the rest of the world. Today, Indian life is slowly changing.

Flooded rain-forest path

How much rain falls in the Amazon rain forest?

A lot! In the wettest places about 100 inches (250 centimeters) of rain falls in a year. That is more than twice the rainfall of New York City each year. And it's more than six times as much as a year's rainfall in Los Angeles.

In the rain forest the wettest months are called the rainy season. Then heavy rain falls during part of every day. The rest of the year is the "dry" season. But even that is not very dry. It's just less wet.

435

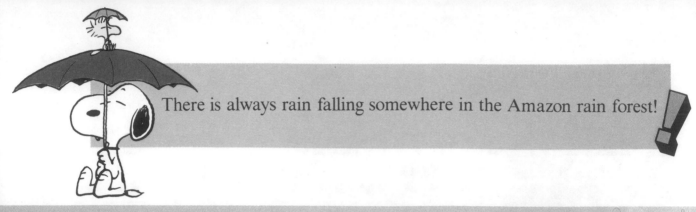

There is always rain falling somewhere in the Amazon rain forest!

What kind of houses do Amazon Indians build?

Some Indians build houses that look like haystacks. These are made of dried palm leaves or dried grasses. A frame of thin poles holds the "hay" in place.

Other Indians use the dried palm leaves for roofs only. They make the walls of their houses from either thin tree trunks or mud.

What's the inside of a rain forest house like?

Each house has one very big room. The floor is a natural dirt floor. The room has some stools made from tree trunks. It has hammocks to sleep in. There are no windows, so the house is dark. Sometimes the Indians build a fire inside to cook their food. But most of the time they do their cooking outdoors.

Who lives in each house?

In many Amazon houses parents, children, grandparents, aunts, and uncles all live together. Sometimes as many as 70 people live in one house! Each set of parents and young children has a part of the big room to themselves.

What do rain forest people eat?

They eat many kinds of fruits and vegetables. They grow some in their gardens and gather some in the forest. They add to their diet by hunting and fishing.

Corn and cassava (kuh-SAH-vuh) are the most important crops in the Amazon rain forest. (Cassava is the plant from which tapioca pudding is made.) The Indians make cakes from dried and grated cassava roots. They roast corn, and they make a soup of ground corn. The Indians also raise and eat sweet potatoes.

Trees of the forest supply the Indians with fruit and nuts. Bees provide them with honey. Some tribes are always on the lookout for a tree with a bee's nest in it. When they see one, they chop it down. They build a smoky fire near the tree to drive the bees away. Then they take the honey from the nest. They eat it, and they drink it mixed in water.

Amazon Indians also eat wild pigs, monkeys, armadillos (are-muh-DILL-oze), turtles, and many kinds of fish. They usually roast the meat and fish over an open fire, barbecue style.

Amazon Indians carrying racks of live turtles to another village

Amazon waters have piranha (pih-RAHN-yuh) fish in them. One piranha can fit in your hand. But a group of piranhas could eat you up in just a few minutes!

Do the Amazon Indians hunt with guns?

Yes. Sometimes they use shotguns to hunt large ground animals. But for hunting birds, fish, and other small animals the Indians stick to their old ways. They use spears, blowguns, or bows and arrows.

A blowgun is a long, hollow bamboo pole. Through it an Indian blows poison darts.

The Indians are very skilled hunters. They can hit fast-moving animals with their arrows and darts. They can even hit fish with their arrows!

Rain forest hunters use bamboo stems to make long arrows. Sometimes the arrow tips are made from the wood of a palm tree. Some bows are as long as 6 feet (2 meters). They may be longer than the hunter! The hunter makes his bow strings from thin strips of palm wood.

HERE'S THE WORLD-FAMOUS HUNTER ON A MOTH CHASE!

Some Amazon Indians hunt at night with the help of modern flashlights!

Is it true that rain forest Indians are unfriendly?

Some of them are. In the past, hunters and explorers hurt and killed many of them. In the early 1900s some were forced to work as slaves by people who came to take rubber from the forest's rubber trees. Because of these things, some Indians dislike strangers.

Other Amazon Indians are shy rather than unfriendly. They are frightened by visitors, who are very different from themselves. Often, though, these Indians learn to trust visitors and accept them as friends.

Man standing by pool with bow and arrow

Tribal chief wearing special ornaments

Is it true that Amazon Indians wear no clothes?

Many rain forest Indians wear little or no clothing. Some wear only belts, armbands, jewelry, or headbands. Some wear only tiny skirts called loincloths.

For special occasions these Indians paint their bodies with dyes made from jungle plants. They use many different colors and designs. Some of the designs stand for animals of the rain forest.

Child wearing beads and feathers

Man dressed for a festival

Amazon mask and costume

439

Who teaches the rain forest children?

Mostly parents, friends, relatives, and older children. But they don't teach reading, writing, and arithmetic. Instead, children learn skills they will need when they grow up. Girls learn how to search for honey and fruit, plant crops, and cook. They also practice weaving cloth and caring for younger children. Boys learn to hunt and fish.

There are a few modern schools in the Amazon rain forest today. They were set up by the government of Brazil. In these schools, children read books and take tests—just as you do.

Do Amazon children have time for toys?

Yes, they do. But they have to make their own. Sometimes their parents help them. They use cornstalks, bits of wood, bones—whatever they can find. They turn these things into dolls, toy animals, and balls.

 In an Indian relay race each man who runs carries a 100-pound (45-kilogram) log on his shoulders!

What happens when people get sick in the rain forest?

Many Amazon Indians believe that evil spirits cause illness. When these Indians are sick, they call in a shaman (SHAY-mun). Shamans are very important people in a rain forest village. They are supposed to be able to see and control evil spirits. Shamans try to drive evil spirits out of a sick person's body to make the person well.

For a long time scientists didn't believe a shaman could really cure a sick person. But most have changed their minds. Doctors and dentists now use as medicines many of the plants shamans have used for a long time.

Jungle villages do not have modern doctors and nurses. However, doctors and nurses sometimes visit the rain forest to take care of sick Indians. The doctors are Brazilians. But they are not Indians. However, there are now some Indian nurses and medical teams.

How People Live in Very Cold Lands

Eskimos of the Arctic

What are the coldest places in the world?

The Arctic (ARK-tick) and the Antarctic (ant-ARK-tick). The Arctic is the area around the North Pole. It is usually colder than the inside of your home freezer! During an arctic winter the temperature sometimes goes as low as −60°F. (−51°C.).

The Antarctic is the snow-and-ice-covered land around the South Pole. It's even colder than the Arctic—so cold that temperatures there have to be measured on special thermometers.

The Arctic and the Antarctic are called the polar regions.

442

Does anyone live in the world's coldest places?

Some birds, seals, fish, whales, insects, and spiders live in parts of the Antarctic. But no people do. Scientists from a few countries sometimes visit there to learn more about the area. But they usually stay less than a year. People do live in the Arctic. They are called Eskimos (ES-kuh-moze). About 50,000 Eskimos live in northern Canada, Alaska, and on the island of Greenland. Maybe 1,500 more live in the arctic areas that belong to Russia.

There are about 120 times as many people in New York City as there are Eskimos in the whole world!

Is there a summer in the Arctic?

Yes. But summer never gets very hot—not even in the southern parts of the Arctic, where it is the warmest. The average summer temperature there is only as warm as spring in Chicago, Illinois. That's about 50°F. (10°C.). And the temperature often drops below freezing. Snow sometimes falls during the summer. In the southern part of the Arctic, the summer snow melts fairly soon. But the ground is always frozen below the surface. This frozen area is called the permafrost.

Only strong plants can grow during the short, cool arctic summer. In spite of this, there are several hundred different kinds of arctic plants.

 Eskimos make a natural freezer by simply digging a hole in the ground.

DON'T TELL ME...LET ME GUESS.....IT SNOWED LAST NIGHT!

WOODSTOCK! I WONDER WHAT HAPPENED TO WOODSTOCK!

POOR WOODSTOCK DOESN'T KNOW HOW TO TAKE CARE OF HIMSELF IN EMERGENCIES...

HE'S PROBABLY SNOWED UNDER, OR FROZEN STIFF, OR...

How do Eskimos keep warm?

By bundling up. In winter they wear warm fur clothing and sleep under fur blankets.

In very cold weather Eskimos put on two of everything. They wear the fur of the first layer of clothing against their skin. They wear the fur of the second layer on the outside.

An Eskimo wears fur boots called mukluks (MUCK-lucks). Their outer soles are made from the skin of a moose or seal. Their tops are made from canvas or caribou (KAR-uh-boo) skin. A caribou is a kind of deer that lives in the Arctic.

In an igloo, an Eskimo family sleeps on a bed made of snow blocks!

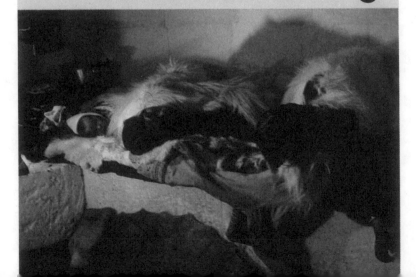

Do all Eskimos live in igloos?

No. In fact, very few modern Eskimos live in them. But most know how to build igloos from snow blocks. Only in Canada do some Eskimos still live in igloos for most of the year. During the short summer, they move into tents made from animal skins.

Most Eskimos today build houses of stone or wood. There is plenty of rock in the Arctic. So building stone is easy to get. But wood is hard to find and expensive to buy. Trees cannot grow in the Arctic because of the cold and the permafrost. Eskimos who live near water often collect and use driftwood that washes up on the shore. It is carried by the ocean from places south of the Arctic. Other Eskimos buy logs or boards for their houses. They are brought by ship from faraway places. That's why they are so expensive.

Modern houses with electricity and oil furnaces are recent. They mark a great change in the lives of the Eskimo people.

445

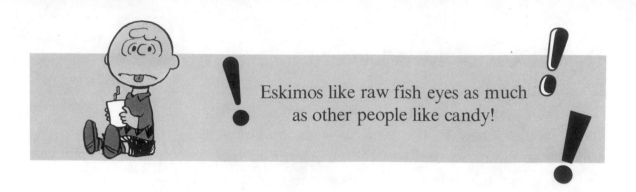

Why don't igloos melt when Eskimos cook their food?

Because cooking doesn't produce enough heat. An Eskimo family that lives in an igloo uses a small saucer-shaped lamp as a stove. It burns animal fat and gives off enough heat to cook meat and fish. It even gives off enough heat to make the igloo a little warmer. But the temperature inside the igloo stays below freezing. So the snow blocks can't melt. The Eskimos must wear their fur clothing inside the igloo.

Some Eskimos use their lamps for warmth and light only. They eat their food raw.

446

How do Eskimos travel in the snowy Arctic?

Like many things in Eskimo life, travel is a mixture of the old and the new.

At one time Eskimos did all of their traveling in sleds pulled by dogs. Some Eskimos still travel this way. But many use snowmobiles with gasoline engines instead.

For travel on water, Eskimos use motorboats, kayaks (KIE-aks), and umiaks (OO-mee-aks). Both kayaks and umiaks are made of animal skins stretched over a wooden frame. Eskimos move them by paddling.

For long trips Eskimos often travel by airplane. Small planes fly regularly between many places in the Arctic. Some planes use skis instead of wheels for landing and taking off.

Eskimo sled

Eskimos and sled dogs watching approach of an airplane

Kayaks

Snowmobiles pulling sleds across ice

Do Eskimos have doctors and dentists?

Yes, they have both. In the past, few doctors and dentists were Eskimo. But that is changing. More and more young Eskimos are studying medicine and dentistry. They go to school in the United States, Canada, or Denmark.

In most Eskimo villages, there is no permanent doctor's or dentist's office. About once a month a doctor travels by airplane to visit a village. The doctor sets up an office in a government building. People from that village and nearby smaller ones come to the office. After a day or two, the doctor leaves. Dentists visit in the same way.

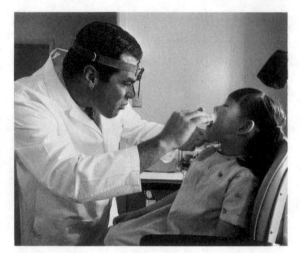

When Eskimos are very sick, an airplane takes them to a hospital. Modern Eskimos have better health care than they ever did. Yet, they are not as healthy as they used to be. Visitors to the Arctic have brought germs that make Eskimos sick. Some of the modern food that Eskimos buy harms their teeth. So arctic doctors and dentists have plenty of patients.

Do all Eskimos hunt and fish?

No, not anymore. Until just a short time ago, all Eskimo men were hunters and fishers. The only ways Eskimos could get meat and fish were by hunting and fishing. And these were also the only ways Eskimos could get skins for clothing, blankets, and boats.

Today, they can buy most things at stores or through mail-order catalogues. Those Eskimos who supply stores need to be hunters or fishers. Most others don't. They do other kinds of work. Some run small stores. Some are guides for arctic travelers. Others have different jobs. But most Eskimo men still hunt and fish for sport. Seal and caribou are hunted most often.

Are there schools for Eskimo children?

Yes, but only in large villages. Children who live in small villages must leave their families to get an education. When they are ready to start first grade, they move to a village that has a school. Children from a few villages live together in a large building. Usually there are fewer than 30 children. At the end of the school year, they go home.

What games do Eskimos play?

Eskimos spend much of their playtime indoors, where they can keep warm. Children spend hours playing cat's cradle. Both adults and children play dominoes and a few kinds of card games. They also enjoy a game that is something like darts. They hang caribou antlers from the ceiling. Then they try to throw sticks through manmade holes in the antlers.

But the cold weather doesn't keep Eskimos from playing outdoor games, too. Naturally, the games are played in the snow or on ice. Ice hockey is a favorite. Eskimos sometimes make the puck from a walrus tusk. Long walrus bones make good hockey sticks to hit the puck with. Eskimo children like to speed downhill on sleds. Their parents enjoy dog-sled and snowmobile racing.

How People Live in the Mountains

People of the Himalayas

What is the tallest mountain in the world?

Mount Everest. It is 5½ miles (about 9 kilometers) high! That's almost 20 times as tall as the Empire State Building in New York City.

Mount Everest is one of many high peaks in Asia's Himalaya (him-uh-LAY-uh) Mountains. In that great mountain chain there are 92 peaks more than 4 miles (about 6 kilometers) high.

IF HE TRIES TO INSTALL A CABLE CAR AND A SUMMIT RESTAURANT, I'M LEAVING!

In what country are the Himalayas?

The Himalayas stretch across more than one country. Within this great mountain chain are three whole countries—Nepal (nuh-PAWL), Sikkim (SICK-im), and Bhutan (boo-TAHN). The Himalayas also reach into India, Pakistan, and Tibet. The Himalayas are as long from end to end as the distance between New York City and Miami, Florida.

Although the Himalayan peoples live in different countries, they are alike in many ways. They share the same kind of mountain life.

Who lives in the Himalayas?

About 20 million people live in the Himalayas. Most of them live in small villages tucked away in narrow strips of land between high mountains. We call these places valleys.

Himalayans have dark straight hair, dark eyes, and brown skin. They are short people, but most of them are strong.

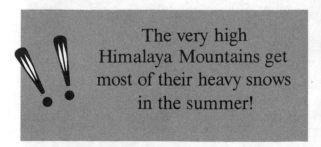

The very high Himalaya Mountains get most of their heavy snows in the summer!

Himalayan village

What are Himalayan houses like?

Most Himalayan houses are made of stone. Because glass is expensive, there are few windows. The houses stay warmer this way, too. Some houses have flat roofs. Others have roofs with a slight slant. Himalayans lay heavy stones on top of both kinds of roofs. The stones keep the roofs from blowing off in the strong mountain winds which blow all the time.

Himalayan houses are small. But they have two or three floors. The third floor is used to store food and hay. More food and wood is stored on the ground floor. In the winter it becomes a barn for animals, too. The second floor of the house has one big room. This is where the Himalayan family lives.

In cold weather the family gathers around an open fire. The fire keeps them warm and cooks their food. But the fire fills the room with smoke because Himalayan houses have no chimneys. Instead, smoke slowly escapes through the roof. No one seems to know for sure why the Himalayans have no chimneys. But we do know that they don't seem to mind the smoky air in their houses. Sometimes, though, it makes their eyes burn.

What animal is the Himalayan's best friend?

The yak is the Himalayan's best friend. It is a big animal that looks like a buffalo. Because yaks can live in rugged mountain areas, Himalayans use them for many things.

Yaks pull plows for Himalayan farmers. They can be ridden like horses, and they can carry heavy loads. Mountain women weave the yak's long hair into cloth for blankets and clothing. Yak hide, with the hair taken off, makes warm, sturdy boots.

Even the yak's horns and tail are useful. Horns are turned into musical instruments. Himalayans brush away flies with what was once a yak's tail.

The yak also supplies mountain people with meat and milk.

While looking for grass to eat, yaks have climbed close to the top of Mount Everest!

YOU BETTER SHAPE UP... YOU COULD BE REPLACED BY A YAK!

YAK! YAK! YAK!

How do Himalayans earn a living?

Some Himalayans raise sheep, goats, or yaks. A few work as guides for tourists and mountain climbers. But most are farmers. They raise cereal crops such as barley and wheat on the mountain slopes. They also grow fruits and vegetables in the valleys near their homes. Most farmers also have one or two goats, yaks, oxen, or sheep.

Yak

Couple removing dirt and husks from grain

What do Himalayan people eat?

These mountain people eat the cereal and other crops that they raise. Barley, for example, is roasted, then ground, and made into bread. Boiled or fried potatoes are a favorite food.

Yak meat is eaten fresh, or after it has been dried. Yak meat is a treat to Himalayans. They don't have it often, since they like to keep their yaks alive as long as possible. Yaks are not killed for meat until they are old. By then their meat is hard to chew. But it's a nice change from sheep and goat meat, which Himalayans eat more often.

Himalayans drink yak milk, and they make cheese and butter from it. Himalayans of all ages drink tea to which salt and yak butter have been added.

Do Himalayans have stores?

Most Himalayan villages do not have stores. The village families grow or make most of the things they need.

Once a year a Himalayan family may travel to a market town. There people from all over the mountain area gather to buy and sell. Some markets are outdoors. Others are in a building.

Family members take with them the sweaters, blankets, and other things they have made. At the market they trade for whatever they need. That might be tea, spices, or metal tools. Because they trade one thing for another, many mountain people do not use money.

454

Woman weaving cloth to take to the market

Do Himalayan children go to school?

Some do and some don't. Only large villages and towns have schools. The mountains make it impossible for children to travel back and forth from one village to another every day. Children from small villages must leave home for a while to go to school. But not very many do. So a lot of children never learn to read and write. Instead they learn to plant crops, weave, cook, and do other practical things. Children from large towns learn reading, writing, and arithmetic, and some go on to college in other countries.

Himalayan school children

How do Himalayan people travel from place to place?

They usually walk. They walk even when they are going to a place many miles away. Building a road across a high mountain is very hard. So few roads have been built in the Himalayas.

Mountain travelers walk along steep, rocky trails. They cross rivers on rickety bridges. Sometimes travelers have to go through a narrow pass, or opening, between mountain peaks. They can do this only when the snow is not very deep.

When they travel, mountain people carry whatever they need for the trip. If they have many bundles, they load them on yaks or other animals.

Travelers walking through the snow

What do Himalayan people do if they get sick?

Many Himalayans believe that illness is caused by evil spirits. When these Himalayans are ill, they call in a shaman. This shaman is much like the shaman of the Amazon rain forest. Both try to cure sickness by dealing with spirits as well as natural medicine.

Himalayans believe that a shaman can ask good spirits to drive out evil spirits. Then the sick person should get well. But sometimes he doesn't. Then the Himalayans say the evil spirits were stronger than the good spirits.

Many Himalayans who live in small isolated villages never visit a modern doctor. As a result, some of them die of diseases a doctor could cure.

Shaman dancing

456

Is there really an "Abominable Snowman"?

Nobody knows for sure. There have been many reports of a shaggy creature who lives in the Himalayas. The creature is reported to be half human and half ape. Some people say it has a high-pitched scream and a bad smell. Its feet are supposed to point backward. The Himalayans' name for the Abominable Snowman is yeti (YET-ee).

The mysterious yeti is said to roam the Himalayas at night. A few people claim to have seen a yeti. But they cannot prove that they did see one. Others claim that they have seen yeti tracks in the snow. But we can't be sure that a yeti made the tracks.

Maybe one day mountain climbers will capture a yeti. Or perhaps they will be able to take a picture of one. Then we will know for sure if the yeti really exists.

Instead of celebrating their real birthdays,
all people in the country of Bhutan become
a year older on New Year's Day!

How People Live in the Desert
People of the Sahara

What is a desert?

A desert is an area of very dry land. Rain almost never falls there. Only a few plants can grow in a desert, and animals have a hard time finding water to drink.

Most deserts are hot and sandy. But others are rocky and cold.

There are deserts in many parts of the world.

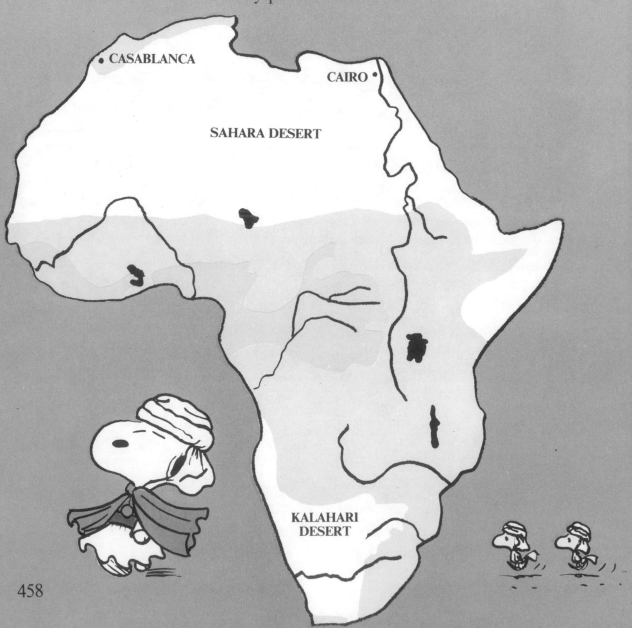

CASABLANCA

CAIRO

SAHARA DESERT

KALAHARI DESERT

What is the world's biggest desert?

The Sahara (suh-HARE-uh) Desert in Northern Africa. It is about the same size as the United States.

Sahara means both "desert" and "wilderness" in Arabic—the language of some of the Saharan people. A wilderness is a place that people have not yet changed and used. The modern Sahara Desert has some towns, highways, factories, mines, and oil fields. But most of it is still a wilderness. So living there is very hard.

Some parts of the Sahara are sandy. Other parts are rocky. But all parts of it are hot and sunny during the day and cool at night.

Saharan sand dunes

! Thousands of years ago the Sahara area wasn't a desert. Old drawings in Saharan caves show people in canoes! !

Who lives in the Sahara Desert?

There are three tribes of people that live in the Sahara. The Moors live in the west. The Tuareg (TWAH-reg) live in the central part. The Tebu (TEH-boo) live in the east.

Each tribe speaks a different language and has its own customs. But because they all live in the desert, their way of life is much the same.

How do desert people get water?

From an oasis (oh-AY-sis). Even a desert has underground water in some places. These places are called oases. At oases the water may rise to the surface and form a spring or water hole. If it doesn't, people can dig a well to reach the water. In the Sahara Desert there are 90 big oases.

Before desert people leave an oasis, they fill goatskin bags with water. Some also fill round rubber tubes found inside old car and truck tires. In this way they have water while they travel.

How do desert people get food?

Some people live at an oasis and grow crops for food there. They use ditches or pipes to run water from a well or spring to the crops. This system is called irrigation (ir-uh-GAY-shun).

Other desert people travel from one spot in the desert to another. They raise herds of animals for meat and clothing. They buy fruits and vegetables at a market whenever they pass through a town. These people are called nomads.

Why do nomads travel from one spot to another?

Most nomads keep traveling to find food and water for their herds of camels, sheep, or goats.

Animals quickly eat the few plants that grow in a desert pasture. Then the nomads have to find a new pasture—sometimes miles and miles away. To reach it they have to travel for at least two days. Sometimes they must travel for two weeks! When they get to a new pasture, they unpack and set up a camp. But soon they will move on again.

Nomads on their way to a new camp

How do nomads carry all their supplies?

On the backs of their camels. Camels are great helpers to desert nomads. Camels' soft, wide feet don't sink deeply into sand. So they can walk easily in the desert. Camels can carry heavy loads. They can also go without drinking water for a long time. Seven to ten days is about their limit when traveling across the desert. And when there is little food, camels can live on the fat that is stored in their humps.

Because camels are good at carrying supplies, some desert people use them to make a living. The camels carry supplies across the desert to be sold. People who sell things are called merchants. Desert merchants often travel together in groups called caravans (CARE-uh-vanz). A caravan of merchants can protect its members against robbers better than a few people traveling alone can.

In the winter, a camel that does not work or travel can go without water for as long as two months!

 HMM... MY ICE CUBES ARE MELTING....

How else do camels help desert people?

Camels not only CARRY supplies—they ARE supplies themselves! Nomads drink camel's milk and eat camel meat. From camel skins, nomads make leather for tents. From camel's hair they make wool clothes.

Camels also carry people on their backs. When desert travelers are tired, they can saddle up a camel like a horse. Then they can ride across the dessert.

Camel loaded with supplies

Do nomads take their houses with them when they move?

Yes! Most nomads live in tents made of camel skins. The tents are held up with poles. Some nomads make their own poles from trees found at oases. Other nomads buy theirs from passing caravans. At moving time, they fold up their tents. They can then easily load the tents onto camels.

The objects in nomad houses get packed up, too. Nomads don't use the same kind of furniture as we do. Chairs, tables, and beds are heavy and bulky. A camel couldn't carry them around the desert easily. Instead, nomads use mats that they weave from palm branches. Nomads sit on mats, sleep on mats, and use mats as tables.

Nomad family sitting on mats in front of their tent

 From years of walking through sand, the soles of nomads' feet become tough. Some can put their feet in a low fire and not feel it!

Do nomads take baths while traveling across the desert?

No! Traveling nomads must use all the water they have for drinking and cooking. They have to wait until they settle at another oasis before they can take a bath. This can sometimes be as long as two weeks.

Desert market

Are there towns in the Sahara?

Yes, but most of them are small. And all are near water.

In a desert town, people live in houses made from mud bricks dried in the sun. At the center of the town is usually an outdoor market. There the people buy food and supplies. Some larger desert towns also have stores, restaurants, and hotels.

Nomads sometimes travel to a desert town to visit the market. There they often sell or trade some of their animals. Sometimes they spend time with friends who live in the town.

Do nomads go to school?

Some do. Many of the governments of Saharan countries send teachers to nomad camps. So people learn to read and write.

Boy learning to read

464

What kind of food is served at a desert meal?

When desert families have guests, they often serve sheep or lamb that has been roasted over an open fire. On ordinary days, desert cooks boil the meat of a sheep, a lamb, or a chicken. Chickpeas and cut-up vegetables such as carrots, onions, and beans go into the same pot. Cooks also add pepper and other spices. A desert family eats a cereal called couscous (KOOS-koos), too. It is usually served in a large bowl with the meat and vegetables.

Family eating millet

Camel cheese and camel butter are also popular foods. Camel cheese is made from camel's milk. But camel butter isn't. Camel butter is the fat from the camel's hump. People smear it on certain foods. Or else they dip their fingers in it and eat it plain.

Desert people like to drink sweet tea with their meals. But sometimes they drink goat's milk or camel's milk.

 A pile of sand formed by the wind is called a sand dune. There is one in the Sahara Desert that is taller than the highest building in New York City!

Is all of the Sahara covered with sand?

No. Most of the Sahara Desert does NOT have sand on it! In some areas tiny pebbles called gravel cover the ground. In other places there is only bare rock. The middle of the big desert has the most sand.

Is there anything under the sand and rock of the Sahara?

Yes. Oil! Oil companies have found large amounts of valuable oil under the sand and rock of Algeria (al-JEER-ee-uh) and Libya (LIB-ee-uh). Algeria and Libya are two countries in the northern part of the Sahara Desert.

Oil companies have started bringing up the oil from under the desert. Pipe lines carry the oil from the desert to African cities on the Mediterranean (med-ih-tuh-RAY-nee-un) Sea. This sea is just north of Africa.

From the cities the oil is loaded into big ships called tankers. It is then shipped to places all over the world. Some of it comes to the United States.

Has oil changed life in the Sahara Desert?

Yes. Many Libyans and Algerians have stopped living as nomads. They now work in the oil fields. Instead of moving from place to place, they live in new towns near their jobs.

Because of the oil business, roads have been built across the desert. Trucks carry some of the loads that camels once carried.

But in the rest of the Sahara Desert, life goes on as it has for many hundreds of years.

How People Live in the Lowlands
The Rice Farmers of Asia

Which is the most commonly eaten food in the world?

Charlie Brown is right. More people eat rice than any other food. It is the main food of about half the world's people.

In Asia, rice is one food that almost everybody eats. Asians depend on rice for starches that give their bodies energy.

Where does rice grow?

Rice grows in warm, wet places, including the southern part of the United States. Usually land good for growing rice is low. More rice is grown in Asia than anywhere else. China, India, Indonesia (in-duh-NEE-zhuh), Bangladesh (BANG-luh-desh), Japan, and Thailand (TIE-land) are the six Asian countries that grow the most rice.

Do many people live in the six main rice-growing countries of Asia?

Yes. Nearly two billion people live there. This is slightly less than half the people in the whole world! And the number of people in these countries is growing very fast. In some areas there, people are already terribly crowded together.

468

How can people find enough land to farm in such crowded places?

Most of Asia's rice growers farm small pieces of land. The land on which rice grows is called a paddy. Some paddies are no bigger than a football field.

But there are many of these small paddies. Together they produce a lot of rice. The six main rice-growing countries produce about 260 million tons (236 million metric tons) of rice a year.

Paddy means "rice field." So when you say "rice paddy" you are saying "rice-rice field."

HOW WOULD IT SOUND IF I CHANGED MY NAME TO PATTY RICEFIELD OR RICE PATTYFIELD OR RICE RICEFIELD OR...

GOOD GRIEF!

What animal helps Asians grow rice?

The water buffalo. It is a large, strong animal with big horns. In spite of its size, the water buffalo is a gentle animal. A child can safely lead one as it works.

When a rice farmer plows his paddy, a water buffalo usually pulls the plow. The plow makes ditches in the earth. Then rice seeds are planted in them. From the seeds, stalks grow a few feet high. On the stalks grow the grains which people eat. When the grains are ripe, the stalks are cut down. They are put on a cart that is pulled by a water buffalo. The stalks are then spread on the ground. The water buffalo walks over them. This forces the grains from the stalks.

Water buffalo pulling plow in Indonesia

469

Do rice farmers use any farm machines?

Most paddies are too small for the rice farmer to use farm machines. Instead, the work is done by hand. All the family members help to plant the rice and pull weeds from the paddy. When the rice is ripe, they cut it with sharp knives.

A few rice farmers have begun to use tractors to pull their plows. Because the paddies are so small, a few families share one tractor. But even these families do most of their work with their hands.

Flooded rice fields in the Philippines

Rice is grown in flooded fields.
This means that the rice farm
family often works in ankle-deep water!

How do rice farmers flood their fields?

Water to flood rice fields usually comes from rivers. Man-made waterways called canals carry the water to narrow ditches. The ditches carry the water to the paddies. Farmers build gates of wood or mud to stop the flow when enough water is in the paddy. Dikes hold the water in. Dikes are low walls made from the soil of the paddy. Most rice-growing areas have a lot of rain during the growing season. This makes it easier to keep the paddies flooded. But from time to time, the farmer has to add more water anyway.

470

Farmers cleaning rice grains

 Some Indonesian people believe that rats and mice brought rice to their land. So they let these animals eat as much rice from the fields as they like!

HEY, STUPID CAT, HOW DOES THAT GRAB YOU?

What kind of houses do Asian rice farmers build?

Many build houses high up on stilts. This keeps them from being flooded during heavy rains. The stilts and the walls of the houses are made of wood or bamboo. The roofs are made of straw or strips of metal.

Most houses are small. Sometimes they have only one room. But almost every house has a porch.

The houses have windows—but no glass or screens. The rice farmers are poor and cannot afford them. So insects fly right inside the houses. And there are many flies, mosquitoes, and other insects in the rice-growing countries. During bad weather the people cover their windows with wooden shutters.

Where do rice farmers build their houses?

Rice farmers build their houses in villages. They do not live right next to their fields as American farmers do. Each morning the rice farmers walk from the village to their paddies. At the end of the day they walk home again.

In some rice-growing areas there are few roads. Rivers and canals go to more places than roads do. Many rice farmers live in villages close to a river or canal. These people usually travel in a rowboat.

471

Rice farmers who live near a canal use its waters for bathing, cooking, brushing their teeth, and washing their clothes!

Philippine school children working in field next to their school

Japanese teacher helping child with his writing

Are there schools for rice farmers' children?

Only in some places. In China and Japan there are schools for the children of ALL rice-farming families. But in the other leading rice-growing countries, only the largest villages have schools. In some places teachers or older students visit middle-sized villages for a few months at a time. They teach children to read, write, and do arithmetic. But many children who grow up in small, poor villages never learn to read and write.

472

Where do rice farmers go shopping?

In the nearest town. Few small villages have stores of their own.

For some rice-growing families, going shopping means taking a boat ride on a river or a canal. For other families it means walking a few miles. In some places they can ride at least part of the way in a small bus.

Families often take along something to sell at the town market.

Shoppers in Thailand traveling by boat to stores that line the canals

What do rice farmers eat?

It should be no surprise that their main food is rice. Asian rice farmers boil most of the rice that they eat. But they also eat it steamed or fried. Sometimes they cover the rice with a sauce made from boiled fish.

Market in Indonesia

Some rice-growing families also raise and eat sweet potatoes, yams, beans, peas, or other vegetables. They might have a few fruit trees, some chickens, and a pig. Now and then they go fishing, or they buy a fish. But the poorest rice farmers have little to eat besides rice.

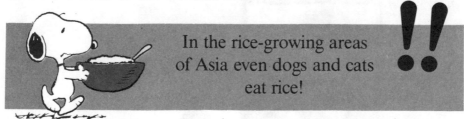

In the rice-growing areas of Asia even dogs and cats eat rice!

473

How healthy is rice?

Rice is full of B vitamins and iron. For a very long time, people in the United States used to throw out the healthiest part of the rice—the bran. The part they ate had none of the vitamins or iron in it.

What we call rice is only part of the rice plant—the grains. Around each rice grain grow a few thin brown coatings called bran. Rice bran is much like the bran used to make bran cereals. But cereal bran comes from wheat—not rice. Around the bran coatings is another coating called the hull. Before people eat rice, they usually take off the bran and the hull. Today, most rice is soaked in hot water before the coatings are taken off. This transfers the vitamins and iron into the white part of the rice grain.

New rice

Ripe rice

Rice grains

Do rice farmers' villages have doctors?

Most villages do not have doctors. A family of rice farmers may live their whole lives without ever visiting a doctor. But some are visited by a shaman.

Many of Asia's rice farmers believe that they are surrounded by spirits. They think that spirits live in every field and every house. To these rice farmers, illness means that the spirits are angry. When they are sick, they do what the Himalayans and Brazilian Indians do. They call in a shaman. He tells them how to make the spirits happy again.

How People Live in the City

What is a city?

A city is a town that has grown very big. Many people live and work there. People usually move to a city from farms and small villages or towns. Some come there to find better or more interesting work. Others come to find more interesting people. Cities often attract people from many different places in the world.

475

Which cities have the most people?

New York City, in the United States, Tokyo (TOE-kee-oh), in Japan, Mexico City, in Mexico, and Shanghai (SHANG-hi), in the People's Republic of China, have the most people. Which of these has the most is hard to say. The numbers keep changing. But more than seven million people live in each of these cities.

Why are many big cities near water?

Long ago there were no cars, trains, or airplanes. There were just a few rough roads for horses and carriages. So the easiest way to travel long distances was by ship.

Cities grew up near oceans and rivers. Travelers got on or off ships there. People could find jobs there. Traders moved there to buy and sell things that ships carried. Some workers moved to cities to make things that were sent away on ships. Others found jobs in hotels, banks, and stores. As a result, the cities grew larger and larger.

Of the world's four largest cities, only Mexico City is not on a river or ocean.

Mexico City

Tokyo

New York City skyline

Why do some cities have subways?

To help people get around the city. Subways carry many people at once. If all these people were driving cars through the city streets, traffic would be jammed up all the time. There would be even fewer parking spaces than there are now.

Subways are electric railways that run through tunnels under some cities. They carry people quickly from one part of the city to another. They are fast because there is no other traffic under the streets. Some subway trains stop every few blocks. So people don't have far to walk when they get off the train. Usually an elevator, a stairway, or a moving stairway called an escalator (ES-kuh-lay-tur) leads from the station to the street.

Sixty-seven of the world's cities have subways. Of these, New York City's subway has the most riders—in some years as many as two billion!

The world's largest apartment building is in London, England. It has apartments for 1,220 families!

BLIMEY!

What kinds of houses are there in a city?

Many city people live in either apartment houses or row houses.

Apartment houses are buildings that have been divided into groups of rooms called apartments. Each apartment is a home for one person or a family. Some apartment buildings are very large. Hundreds of people live in them.

A row house is one in a row of small houses. Usually just one family lives in each house. All the houses are joined together, and they all look alike. The row of houses may be as long as a city block.

Cities have apartment houses and row houses to save space. Cities have a lot of people, but they usually have little land. Everything must be crowded together. Apartment houses take up air space instead of using up more ground space. Row houses use more land than apartment houses. But they use less land than separate one-family houses.

In every city there are at least a few separate houses for one family. These houses usually cost a lot of money.

Which city has the most tall buildings?

New York. There's no way to tell how many tall buildings there are. The number keeps growing all the time.

The Empire State Building was the tallest in New York until the World Trade Center was built. The Trade Center is 1,350 feet (404 meters) high.

How can a city sink?

When water is pumped out from under a city, the city slowly sinks.

The soil under Mexico city has a lot of water in it. The city gets some of its drinking water by pumping it out of the soil. As the water level in the soil gets lower, the soil gets lower too. And so do the streets and buildings on top of the soil.

Parts of Tokyo are also sinking. The sinking areas were once all water. The water was filled in with land to make more room for people to live. Water for factories to use is pumped out from under this man-made land. So the land sinks. These areas are so low that they get flooded whenever there are heavy rains.

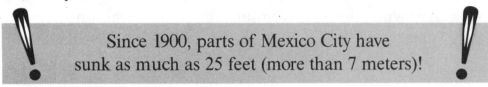

Since 1900, parts of Mexico City have sunk as much as 25 feet (more than 7 meters)!

Which is the oldest city in the world?

Probably Jericho (JER-uh-koe). It is in Jordan near Israel. Groups of people were living there about 7,000 or 8,000 years ago!

If you have heard Bible stories, you probably know something about Jericho. The story is that Joshua and his men surrounded the city. They blew trumpets and yelled until the walls around Jericho tumbled down.

By digging under the earth, scientists have found ruins of Jericho as it was a long time ago.

479

Did all large cities grow from small towns?

Most of them did. But some cities were planned and built as cities. These places were never small towns. They started out big. Factories, stores, apartment buildings, and offices were built as part of the plan.

Planned cities are the easiest to get around in. Streets are laid out neatly. Buildings and stores aren't jumbled together the way they are in many cities that grew without any plan. Planned cities are called new towns. Columbia, Maryland, and Reston, Virginia, are two new towns.

Another example of a planned city is Brasília (brah-SEEL-yuh), in Brazil. It was built to be that country's capital.

Brasília was designed in the shape of a large cross. You can see the cross when you look down at Brasília from an airplane. All around the city are green fields. Wide roads that lead to the city have been built through the fields.

Brasília has the world's widest street.
It is wider than two and a half football fields
placed end to end!

Which is the best city in the world?
There are so many wonderful cities in the world that no one can truly say which is the best.

Did You Know That...

Some people trade or barter for things that they need. They might trade a chicken in exchange for some cloth, or a bushel of apples for an ax. But when most people buy and sell things, they use money. All sorts of things have been used as money—beads, shells, animal skins, feathers, and huge flat stones with holes in the center. Today most people use coins and bills issued by governments. Each country uses its own type of money, with pictures and symbols that have meaning for its citizens. If you traveled to countries all around the world, you would use hundreds of different kinds of bills and coins!

I'LL BARTER ONE KISS FOR TWO JELLY DOUGHNUTS... WHAT DO YOU SAY, SWEETIE?

The first postage stamp was issued in England in 1840. It is known as the "Penny Black," and shows a picture of Queen Victoria. Since that time, stamps have come into common use all over the world. Every country has its own stamp traditions. In the United States no living person is pictured on a stamp. Great Britain is the only country that doesn't put its name on a stamp.

"Penny Black"

Stamp collectors—or philatelists (fih-LAT-uh-lists), as they are called —refer to stamps as "unused" or "used." An unused stamp has not been sent through the mail.

A used stamp has been used as postage and therefore has a cancellation mark on it. Unused stamps are often more valuable.

Stamps vary in value depending on how many of each kind are available and what their condition is. There is only one copy left of a stamp issued by British Guiana in 1856 and it is worth hundreds of thousands of dollars! Printing errors can make stamps valuable. The pictures on about 100 United States air mail stamps were printed upside down. Now each of the stamps is worth tens of thousands of dollars!

Stamps have been used to honor famous people and places, historic events, great works of art, organizations, flowers, and animals.